Rules for children

Never lean on door Always keep all parts car. It is most dangerous to put your head or arms out of the window.

Never touch locks and catches, particularly when the car is moving.

Do not distract the driver; never lean across him or poke him in the back. Try not to make too much noise. Do not expect him to join in your games. It is his job to drive safely.

In addition, look out of the front or back windows or diagonally out of the side windows. If you look straight through the side windows, the objects outside appear to pass more quickly. They will be harder to see clearly and you may begin to feel ill.

Writing, reading and doing things, **in** the car will then be more difficult. If you begin to feel ill, stop that activity and try one looking outside.

Never use such things as knives and scissors when the car is moving. If the car jerks when it goes over a bump or a hole, or if the driver has to brake or stop suddenly, you may injure yourself or someone else.

Travelling by car can be very dull, especially if the journey is a long one and you have to stay inside the car all the time. You will not have much room to play games and you will not be able to take much for your amusement.

There are however many things you can do which will make the journey enjoyable and make the time pass more quickly. In this book you will find lots of ideas to make your travelling interesting, however old or young you are.

Useful Ladybird travelling companions:

Learnabout Maps

Leader: Man and his car

How it works: The Motor Car

Leader: Roads

Leader: Bridges

What to look for inside a Church

What to look for outside a Church

Wild Life in Britain

car games

by DAVID HARWOOD

illustrated by ERIC WINTER *and* MARTIN AITCHISON

Ladybird Books Loughborough

Writing in a car

You will need a firm surface if you wish to write in the car, since you will have to balance it on your knees or hold it in your hand. Here are four suggestions:

1 Use a slate (which is like a small blackboard), and write with chalk. Rub out with a soft damp cloth.

2 Buy a carbon pad from a stationer's or toy shop. You can write on it with a pencil, a ball point pen or any other pointed object. When you wish to rub out, you pull the tab at the bottom and push it in again.

3 Make a special car writing pad by covering a piece of thick white cardboard with a clear material like Fablon or Transpaseal (obtainable from Boots). You can write on this with a chinagraph pencil. When you wish to rub out what you have drawn or written, all you need to do is to wipe the surface with a damp cloth. Do not forget to take a pencil sharpener.

4 Get a piece of wood, hardboard or thick cardboard about 10 cm (4 in) wide and 15 cm (6 in) long. Buy a pad of paper (or make up a pad of scrap paper) and secure it to the backing board with thick elastic bands at the top and at the bottom.

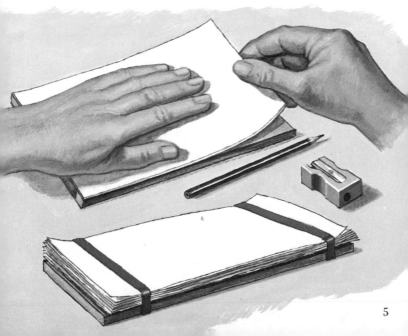

Guessing games

I spy

One person picks something he can see: for example, the windscreen. He does not tell anyone what it is but says: 'I spy with my little eye, something beginning with W.' The others in the car then have to guess what object the challenger has chosen. It is fairer for those who are guessing to ask questions in turn. Whoever gives the correct answer first, has the next go. Remember that everyone who is playing this game must be able to see the object being guessed.

Who am I?

Decide who will have the first go. He then thinks of a person he is pretending to be. The person could be a famous man or woman who could be alive; someone from history, or a relation or a friend. Anyone will do as long as it is possible for everyone in the car to have a chance of getting the answer. The others ask questions in turn, such as 'Are you alive?', and 'Are you a man?' The answers to the questions can be only 'yes' or 'no'. The player who names the person first is the next to ask 'Who am I?'

Henry VIII

Charles I

Michelangelo

Sir Thomas More   *Charlotte Brontë*   *William Shakespeare*   7

Where am I?

This game is played in a similar way to 'Who am I?' but instead of a person you choose a place. It could be a country; a town, city, or village; a well-known building; or somewhere near home like your school, a church, or the shop where your mother buys her meat.

Animal, Vegetable, Mineral or Abstract

One person selects someone or something, and gives only one clue about it. He tells the others whether it is 'animal', 'vegetable', 'mineral', 'abstract', or whatever combination of two or more of the four it is. For example, 'a cabbage' would be *vegetable*; 'Mummy's wedding ring' would be *mineral* (the ring) *with animal connections* (Mummy); 'an idea' would be *abstract*. The others take it in turn to ask questions up to a total of 20. Whoever gets the correct answer gets

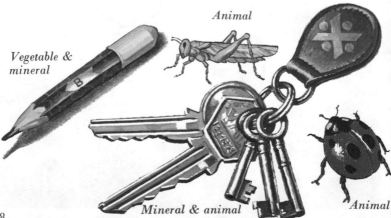

Animal

Vegetable & mineral

Mineral & animal

Animal

Animal

Animal

Vegetable

Mineral

a point and sets the next question. If no one gets the answer after twenty questions have been asked, the person who was being quizzed gets one point and also sets the next question. The winner is the first person to get five points.

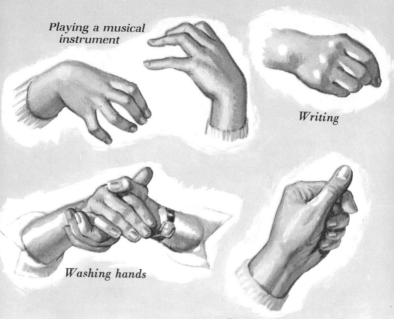

Playing a musical instrument

Writing

Washing hands

Ringing door bell

Mini-mime

Miming is acting without words. There is not very much space inside a car. You will have to be careful not to interfere with the driver in any way and to keep sitting down yourself. Try doing mime using only your hands and see if the others can guess what you are doing. You should not need any 'props' or costumes, but let your hands and fingers or your face do all the acting. It is surprising how many people use their hands in their work. You could decide to mime something which shows a person's job,

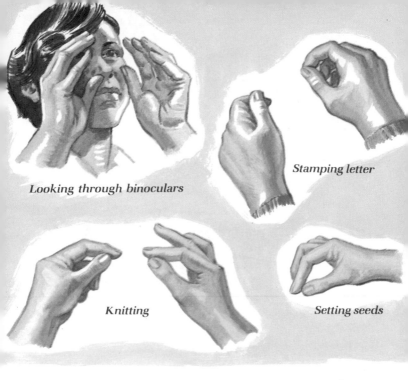

Looking through binoculars

Stamping letter

Knitting

Setting seeds

like playing the piano for a pianist, typing for a typist, or using a paint brush for an artist. You could choose part of someone's job, like weeding for a gardener, sounding someone's chest with a stethoscope for a doctor, counting money for a bank clerk, or putting food on the scales for a shop assistant. There are also lots of things which you do every day which require the use of your hands, like combing your hair, brushing your teeth, tying your tie, turning the pages of a book, writing a letter, knitting, sewing, ringing the door bell or a bicycle bell.

*1947 Hillman Minx
Four door Saloon*

1934 Singer le Mans

1948 Morris Minor

Index marks and registration numbers

Every motor vehicle in the United Kingdom
(with the exception of those belonging to the
Queen) must have a number plate which is
properly called the registration mark.

The registration mark is made up of a series of
numbers and letters. There may be one, two or

three letters followed by one, two, three or four numbers; or the numbers may appear before the letters. The letters in one or two letter marks indicate the area in which the vehicle was first registered. With three letter marks, ignore the first letter; the last two are the guide.

Before October 1974 there were 183 licensing authorities in Great Britain which were county or county borough or borough councils. You will find a list of these in an 'old' AA Handbook or similar publication.

Since October 1974 the registering and licensing of new vehicles in England, Scotland and Wales has been centralised at Swansea, with 81 local licensing offices, each with its own series of index marks. There is a list of these index marks at the back of the book.

Since 1963 an extra single letter has been added at the end of the registration mark: this is called the year-letter suffix. From 1963 to 1966 the letter covered a calendar year, but from 1967 the registration year ran from the 1st August to the 31st July of each year.

A - 1963	J - 1970/71	S - 1977/78
B - 1964	K - 1971/72	T - 1978/79
C - 1965	L - 1972/73	U - missed out
D - 1966	M - 1973/74	V - 1979/80
E - 1967 : to 31st July	N - 1974/75	W - 1980/81
F - 1967/68	O - missed out	X - 1981/82
G - 1968/69	P - 1975/76	Y - 1982/83
H - 1969/70	Q - missed out	Z - missed out
I - missed out	R - 1976/77	

Since August 1983, a letter has been put *before* the number, starting with A, as in A357 FUT.

Games with registration numbers

Counting

Starting at 100, look for a vehicle which has 100 on its number plate. When you have seen it, look for 101, then 102 and so on. It is a game which you can play as long as you like and one which you can continue on many journeys. For example, if you reached 124 on one journey, start at 125 on the next and see how long it takes you to reach 999!

Spot numbers

Each player writes down any five numbers between 1 and 999. They then watch out for their chosen numbers on the vehicles as they pass. As a number on his list is seen the player ticks it off. The first one to have seen all five of the numbers on his list is the winner.

Additions

For these games you need to *add* the numbers in the registration together. For example, 479 would equal 20 (4 + 7 + 9) and 237 = 12. The highest number you could have would be 27 (9 + 9 + 9). Using this addition method you could play the 'counting' and 'spot number' games between 1 and 27; or choose your lucky number (any number between 1 and 27) and see how many times it comes up in, say, a quarter of an hour.

Games with registration letters

The alphabet

Look out for 'year letters' after the numbers, starting with cars registered in 1963, having the letter A, then 1964 models with B, and continuing year by year to the very recent registrations. The letter S was reached in 1977. The letters I, O, Q and U are missed out of year letters.

With two-letter and three-letter registrations, look for groups of letters: for example, DE, ST, BCD, LMN, TUV, but ignoring the 'year' letter at the end, where there is one. Starting at A, see how quickly you can progress to Z. The first plate must be A, AB or ABC. After the first, the next should follow on with the letters continuing in alphabetical order, even if the same letters are repeated like this:

> AB   EF
>
>   BCD FGH
>
>   GHI   JKL

and so on. Again, you may not find I, O, Q or Z.

Abbreviations

An abbreviation is either part of a word written instead of the whole word (for example, m. for metre) or the initial letters of a word or words (for example, VC for Victoria Cross, BBC for British Broadcasting Corporation, IBA for Independent Broadcasting Authority). Most dictionaries contain the meanings of many abbreviations. How many can you identify from the letters on registration plates?

AM 316

Ante Meridiem

DR 999

Bachelor of Arts

BA 421

Doctor

HRH 416

MPS KCB 2

Knight Commander of the Bath

Member of the Pharmaceutical Society

His (or Her) Royal Highness

Rest in Peace

Associate of the Royal Academy

RIP

ARA 716

PMG 525

RHA 58

Post Master General

Royal Horse Artillery

Words

Some letters on registration plates will make up words like CAT, WAS and RUN. Write down those which you see which are words, and when you have five or more words, try and make up a sentence. OUR CAT CAN FLY, for instance.

What is the longest word you can make from the letters you see? Start with the letter or letters from one plate and then add the letter or letters from other plates to the front or the back of the letters you have already written down. Here is an example:

ON 232   ADE 123   LEM 874
= Lem-on-ade

Initials

What are the initial letters of your names? If your name was Simon Alastair Hill, your initials would be S.A.H. If it was Anne Smith, they would be A.S. Look for your initials, those of the others in the car, your friends, teachers, and so on.

The games will be easier if the 'year' letter is not used for playing purposes.

International plates

Every vehicle which is taken abroad from Great Britain has to have a mark like this on the back: **GB**. In the same way, visitors to Britain also have to have a plate on their vehicles which indicates the country from which they come. Here is a list. How many countries can you identify and do you know where each country is located?

A	Austria	D	German Federal Republic	GB	United Kingdom of Great Britain & N. Ireland*
ADN	Yemen, People's Democratic Republic (*formerly* Aden)	DDR	German Democratic Republic	GBA	•Alderney*
		DK	Denmark	GBG	•Guernsey*
AFG	Afghanistan	DOM	Dominican Republic	GBJ	•Jersey*
AL	Albania				•Channel Islands
AND	Andorra	DY	Benin (*formerly* Dahomey)	GBM	Isle of Man*
AUS	Australia*			GBZ	Gibraltar
		DZ	Algeria	GCA	Guatemala
B	Belgium			GH	Ghana
BD	Bangladesh* (*formerly* East Pakistan)	E	Spain (including African Localities and provinces)	GR	Greece
				GUY	Guyana* (*formerly* British Guiana)
BDS	Barbados*	EAK	Kenya*		
BG	Bulgaria	EAT or EAZ	Tanzania* (*formerly* Tanganyika & Zanzibar)	H	Hungary
BH	Belize (*formerly* British Honduras)			HK	Hong Kong*
				HKJ	Jordan
BR	Brazil	EAU	Uganda*		
BRN	Bahrain	EC	Ecuador	I	Italy
BRU	Brunei*	ES	El Salvador	IL	Israel
BS	Bahamas*	ET	Egypt (Arab Republic)	IND	India*
BUR	Burma			IR	Iran
		ETH	Ethiopia	IRL	Ireland*
C	Cuba			IRQ	Iraq
CDN	Canada	F	France (including overseas departments and territories)	IS	Iceland
CH	Switzerland				
CI	Ivory Coast			J	Japan*
CL	Sri Lanka* (*formerly* Ceylon)			JA	Jamaica*
		FJI	Fiji*		
CO	Colombia	FL	Liechtenstein	K	Kampuchea
CR	Costa Rica	FR	Faroe Islands	KWT	Kuwait
CS	Czechoslovakia				
CY	Cyprus*			L	Luxembourg

LAO	Lao, People's Democratic Republic (formerly Laos)	
LAR	Libya	
LB	Liberia	
LS	Lesotho* (formerly Basutoland)	
M	Malta*	
MA	Morocco	
MAL	Malaysia*	
MC	Monaco	
MEX	Mexico	
MS	Mauritius*	
MW	Malawi* (formerly Nyasaland)	
N	Norway	
NA	Netherlands Antilles (Curaçao)	
NIC	Nicaragua	
NL	Netherlands	
NZ	New Zealand*	
P	Portugal	
PA	Panama	
PAK	Pakistan*	
PE	Peru	
PL	Poland	
PNG	Papua New Guinea*	
PY	Paraguay	
RA	Argentina	
RB	Botswana* (formerly Bechuanaland)	
RC	Taiwan (formerly Formosa)	
RCA	Central African Republic	
RCB	Congo (formerly French Congo)	
RCH	Chile	
RH	Haiti	
RI	Indonesia*	
RIM	Mauritania	

RL	Lebanon
RM	Madagascar (formerly Malagasy Republic)
RMM	Mali
RN	Niger
RO	Romania
ROK	Republic of Korea (formerly South Korea)
ROU	Uruguay
RP	Philippines
RSM	San Marino
RU	Burundi
RWA	Rwanda
S	Sweden
SD	Swaziland*
SF	Finland
SGP	Singapore*
SME	Suriname* (formerly Dutch Guiana)
SN	Senegal
SU	Union of Soviet Socialist Republics
SWA or ZA	Namibia* (formerly South West Africa)
SY	Seychelles*
SYR	Syria
T	Thailand* (formerly Siam)
TG	Togo
TN	Tunisia
TR	Turkey
TT	Trinidad and Tobago*
USA	United States of America
V	Vatican City (formerly Holy See)
VN	Viet-Nam (Socialist Republic of)

WAG	Gambia
WAL	Sierra Leone
WAN	Nigeria
WD	Dominica* (Windward Islands)
WG	•Grenada*
WL	•St Lucia* •(Windward Islands)
WS	Western Samoa
WV	St Vincent* (Windward Islands)
YU	Yugoslavia
YV	Venezuela
Z	Zambia* (formerly Northern Rhodesia)
ZA	South Africa*
ZRE	Zaire (formerly Belgian Congo)
ZW	Zimbabwe* (formerly Rhodesia)

Note: *In countries marked with an asterisk the rule of the road is drive on the left; otherwise drive on the right.

Other symbols on vehicles

In addition to an index of registration some vehicles have other badges, marks or plates on them either at the front or the back. Some of these are illustrated below. How many of those can you see? What others are there and what do they mean?

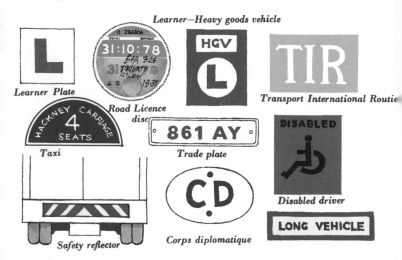

Learner Plate

Road Licence disc

Learner—Heavy goods vehicle

Transport International Routier

Taxi

Trade plate

Disabled driver

Safety reflector

Corps diplomatique

LONG VEHICLE

Trade plates

Trade plates in Britain are issued for the exclusive use of people connected with the motor trade. They consist of **red** numerals and letters on a white background. They are issued by the various licensing authorities and the letters indicate the authority in the same way as normal registration plates.

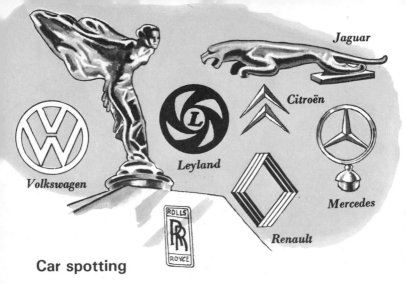

Jaguar

Citroën

Leyland

Volkswagen

Mercedes

ROLLS RR ROYCE

Renault

Car spotting

How many different makes of car can you identify? When you are able to spot makes of car you can then start spotting the various models.

Colours

Everyone playing this game chooses a different colour. When the game starts each person looks for the cars which are the colour he or she has chosen. The first one to reach a score of 20 wins. A different way of playing the game is to write down the different basic colours – RED, WHITE, YELLOW, BLUE, GREEN, BROWN, BLACK – on separate pieces of paper and put them in a 'hat'. Each player takes one piece of paper showing him the colour for which he must look. Two-colour cars do not count.

Policeman • Lieutenant RN • Air Hostess • School Crossing Patrol man

Uniforms

As your car journey progresses, look out for people in uniform. They can be in other vehicles, or they can be walking along the pavement in built-up areas. Many people wear uniforms. Some have uniforms so that everyone will know what jobs they do – for example, a policeman, a traffic warden and a nurse. Other people wear a uniform to show that they are members of a particular voluntary organisation, such as the St John Ambulance Brigade, the British Red Cross Society, the Scouts, the Guides, the Salvation Army, the Automobile Association and the Royal Automobile Club.

Porter

Guardsman

Postman

Nurse

Cub Scout

The men and women serving in the Army, the Royal Navy and the Royal Air Force also wear uniforms. If you are observant you may be able to discover to which particular regiment, branch, ship, etc., the person belongs.

How many different uniforms can you see? Do you know which organisation or job each uniform represents?

If you are travelling on a long journey try and spot any differences in uniform for the same job between one town and another. For example, not all policemen's uniforms are the same.

Means of transport

People travel in many ways, and on your car journey you will be able to look out of the windows not only along the road but further afield as well. On a long car journey you are likely to pass through many different types of country and you will notice many of the ways in which people travel. You could make a list as you go along or have a competition between the passengers, a mark being scored by the first person to name and point to a 'new' form of transport. If it has been counted before, the player loses a mark. Here are some means of transport you may see:

On the pavement Pram, pushchair, wheelchair, child's tricycle, scooter.

On the road Bicycle, tricycle, motor cycle, scooter, lorry, van, bus, coach, tanker, moped, road roller, army vehicles, invalid carriage.

You could – before you start the game – agree to count different types of these. For example, a van could be a post van, a bread van, a milk van and so on, but try not to make the game too complicated.

Beside the road and in the country Horse, cart or trap, tractor, bulldozer or other vehicle with tracks, motor mower with driver's seat, combine harvester.

On the water Remember that you will not have to be on a road which runs beside the sea or a river to spot water transport. You will go over river and canal bridges and may pass close to lakes and reservoirs: ferry, rowing boat, sailing boat, motor boat, dredger, raft, tug, life-raft, barge, rubber dinghy.

In the air Glider, jet aircraft, propeller aircraft, helicopter.

Making things

Knives, scissors, pins, sewing needles, etc., should **never** be used in a moving vehicle, because you could injure yourself if the driver has to brake suddenly. Although you will not have much room in which to work and you will not be able to use many materials, there are many things which you can do without making a mess or getting in the way of the other passengers.

'Plasticine'

This can be made into almost any shape you like. You might find it easier to use if you have a small board which you can rest on your knee as a working surface. Take care to keep the different colours separate so that they can be used again for another model.

Pipe cleaners

You can have lots of fun making people, animals and objects out of the cheapest ordinary pipe cleaners. Most of the enjoyment comes from using your own imagination. The illustrations show you how to make a simple figure. If you want to be more ambitious you can use coloured pipe cleaners; you can bend the cleaners into all sorts of shapes and you can 'dress' the figures with coloured paper, small pieces of material, or ribbon.

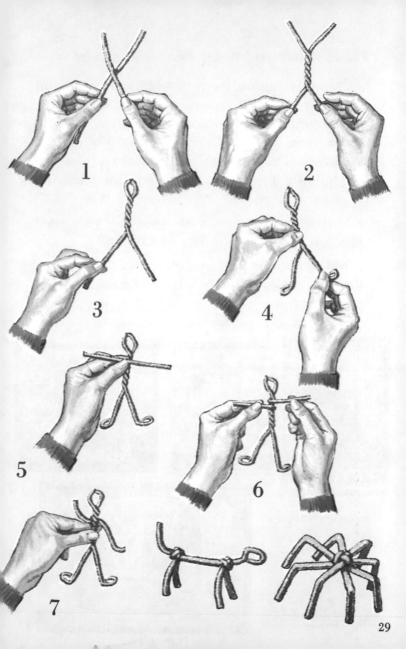

Public house and hotel signs and names

All hotels and public houses have names, and many have an attractive sign hanging up outside. Some of the names are used quite often, like the King's Arms, the Bell or the Plough, but there are others which have most unusual names like the Nobody Inn, the Flowerpot Inn, and the Rhubarb Tavern.

How many different names can you see? Which is the most popular name?

Look at the signs: what picture does each have? How do the signs of hotels and public houses with the same name differ from one another?

The Nobody Inn

30

Tell a story! One person starts telling a story, using the name of a public house or hotel you are passing, to begin. He continues until he spots another hotel or public house, and having brought its name into the tale, lets another passenger take up the story. After a short time the second person passes on the story to a third, and so on for as long as you like.

The game can also be played with the pictures on the signs. Have a look at the nine signs below. Can you make up a story to link them together?

What are the most unusual names for public houses and hotels along part of your route?

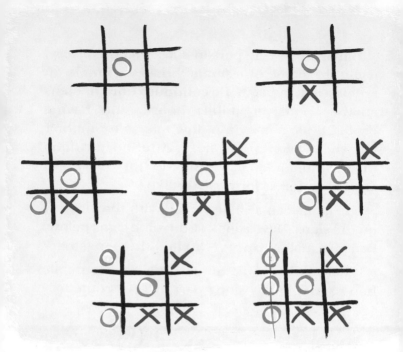

Pencil and paper games

Noughts and crosses

Draw a box as shown in the illustration. One player puts an 'X' in one of the spaces. His opponent then puts an 'O' in another space. The idea is for one player to get a straight row of three 'O's or three 'X's.

Squares

Put an even number of dots (say, 8) in a straight line on a sheet of paper. Add seven more lines of dots underneath the first line. Each dot represents the corner point of a square. Each player takes it in turn to join up two dots with a line. Only one line may be drawn unless the player completes a square, in which case he puts his initial in the square and continues to complete as many squares as he can in the same way. When he can make no more squares he draws another line and passes the sheet on to the next player. When all the dots have been joined, the player with his initial in the most squares is the winner.

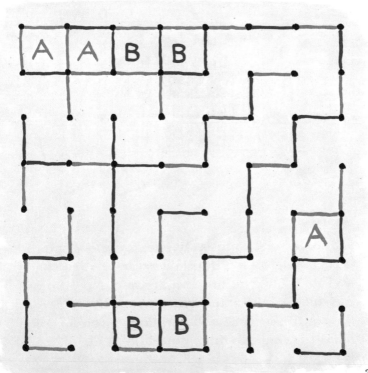

Crosswords

Try making up your own crossword. Do not have too many squares at your first attempts. Black out the blank squares first and then start fitting in the words. You may have to change some words so that they fit in with others. When you have finished, make up the clues, numbering the squares where each word starts. An example is given below.

ACROSS

2
5
6
8

DOWN

1
2
3
4
7

Shapes

One person names a shape – a circle, a square, a rectangle, etc. The players draw that shape and then have a limited time (say, five minutes) in which to draw a picture using the shape as the centrepiece. The illustrations give you some ideas for shapes which could be used.

Circle *Sun* *Watch* *Teapot* *Ladybird* *Balloon*

Square *Window* *Table* *Book* *House* *Television*

Another way to play this game is to give the name of a shape and then to see how many different things you can sketch in a certain number of minutes, using that particular shape.

If more than one person is taking part you can have a competition, the winner being the player with the greatest number of different sketches.

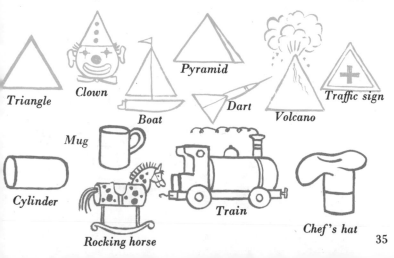

Triangle *Clown* *Boat* *Pyramid* *Dart* *Volcano* *Traffic sign*

Cylinder *Mug* *Rocking horse* *Train* *Chef's hat*

Shopping

Make up a shopping list of all sorts of things which you would like to buy. Include such items as food (meat, fish, vegetables, groceries, etc.), clothes, stamps, books, household requirements, toys, large items (for example, a television set,

an armchair and a bicycle), and so on. When you have completed your list you can play the game in one of two ways.

1 Look at the shops. You are allowed to 'buy' only one item from any one shop. You cannot therefore tick off a lot of items when you pass a supermarket or a large department store. See how long it takes you to 'buy' all the items on your list.

2 Look at the posters on advertisement hoardings. Whenever you see one of the items on an advertisement you can mark it off your list.

Other observation games

There are many other games which you can play by looking out of the window. Here are just a few suggestions:

Flags How many different flags can you spot?

Sports What sports can you see actually being played? What other places can you pick out where a particular sport takes place?

Animals Keep your eyes open not only for pets but also for farm and wild animals. Take different sides of the road and score points – more points for unusual animals.

Memory test

Someone reads a few paragraphs from a newspaper, magazine or book. He then asks questions about the people, places and things mentioned in what he has read. The first person to give the correct answer scores a point or competitors take it in turns to answer.

Table games

A number of popular games which you may play at home like Scrabble and chess are made in special 'travel' versions. Have a look round your toy shop, stationer or department store.

Wordmanship

What is the name of the next major town or city through which your journey will take you? See how many words of three or more letters from it you can write down before you reach its boundary. For example, from EDINBURGH you would get Bin, Red, Rein, Grind.... and many more!

Estimation

Distance Choose a distance of half a mile or a mile. One person acts as judge and only he can look at the car's mileometer.

When the judge gives the signal, each player waits until he thinks that distance has been

covered and says 'now'. The one calling closest to the agreed distance wins.

Time Using a watch with a second hand, one person challenges the others to guess when a given period of time (say 30 seconds) is up. Do not make the period longer than a minute.

Speed Competitors close their eyes and have to estimate the speed of the car when the 'challenger' says 'now'.

Navigating

If you are going on a long journey or visiting a place to which you have not been before, you could, perhaps, help the driver by giving him the correct directions.

Before you leave you could write down the main details of your route. On a long journey by main roads you need only to make notes of the way to get to the first main road, where you will have to make turnings off, and how to reach your destination from the place where you leave a main road.

When you are on the journey keep your eyes open for sign posts and other direction signs, so that you can give the driver the information he requires in plenty of time. You will also have to watch out for diversions, and don't forget that there may have been some new roads or motorways constructed since the map was published.

If part of your journey will be after dark, remember to take a torch, but when you use it keep the beam well away from the driver.

Map reading

When going on a long car journey by main roads you will probably use a **small** scale map. For example, there is less information on a 1:250,000 scale map (approximately ¼″ to the mile) than there is on a 1:50,000 scale map (approximately 1¼″ to the mile). As the scale of the map becomes smaller, the amount of information that can be given grows less. For cross-country journeys, when out for a drive near home, or when on holiday you can have a lot of fun and interest with larger scale maps because they will show everything in much greater detail. You should learn how to read a map so that you know what signs, symbols and other markings on the map represent. The Ladybird book **Learnabout Maps** contains much very useful help and advice about map reading. (A list of Ladybird books of interest when you are travelling will be found opposite the title page.)

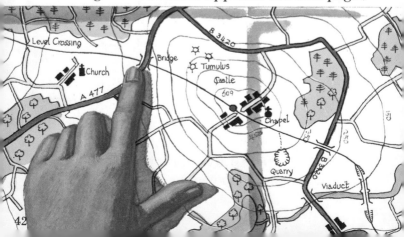

The most popular series of maps for exploring by car is the 1:50,000 (approximately 1¼" to the mile) published by Ordnance Survey. On these you will find all sorts of interesting information and by following your route on the map as you travel you will be able to look for such things as sites of battles, monuments, telephone boxes, milestones, windmills, railways and much more.

A useful hint is to turn the map so that it is always following the direction of the road along which you are travelling.

How are these marked on the map opposite?

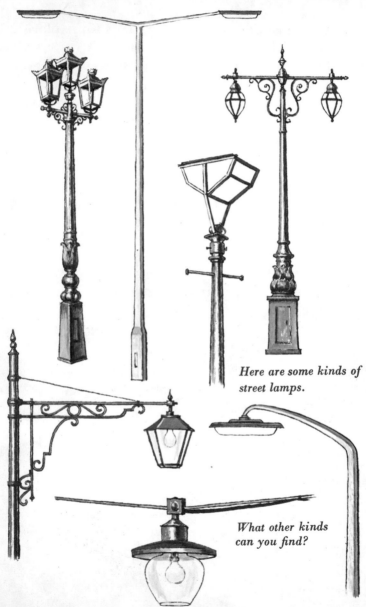

Here are some kinds of street lamps.

What other kinds can you find?

After dark

You can play some of the games and do some of the things already mentioned in this book at night-time as well as during the day. Here are some special suggestions for after dark.

Coloured lights There are lights on vehicles, buildings, illuminated signs, traffic signals and so on. How many different colours of lights can you see?

Street lamps If your route passes through a number of towns and villages make a note of the types of lighting you see. Some examples of street lighting are given on the page opposite.

Noises One person makes a noise (not too loud!) and the others have to guess what the noise represents. Animals and birds will give you plenty of ideas (the purring of a cat, the braying of a donkey, the drilling of a woodpecker, etc.) There are also many other noises which you could make from around the house like the drip of a tap or the click of a light switch.

What's this? The idea of this game is to find out what an object is by using only your sense of touch. One person puts something in a handker-chief, or a paper or thin cloth bag, and it is then passed to the others who have to guess what is inside.

A 400

A 487

Start Here

A 475

B 2776

A 475

A 484

B 2776

46

Finish

A 486

A 487

A 486

B 3048

A 484

A 310

1 Runs

2 Runs

1 Run

1 Run

Car cricket

This game is great fun and is played by two 'teams' each with one or more people. First, each team writes down a list of their eleven players. You will find your car writing board (see page 5) very useful for this. Decide which team is going to bat first. You will not be able to toss a coin as a captain does in a proper game of cricket, but one captain can call 'heads' or 'tails' as the other captain puts a coin on the back of his hand.

The rules of this game are:

1 Only one batsman is in at any one time. He continues to score runs until he is out.

2 There are no overs.

3 Only traffic approaching you from the opposite direction (the oncoming traffic) is allowed.

Runs

6 Runs

Caught out

Bowled out

Out – stumped

Out L.B.W.

4 The illustrations show which vehicles score runs and which put a batsman 'out'.

5 When the first batsman is out, the second goes in and so on until the whole team is out. The other team then goes in.

6 When both teams have played, add up the scores and see who has won – unless you have decided it is to be a two-innings match.

You can, of course, make up your own methods of scoring and add such things as 'rain stopped play', 'bad light stopped play' and so on.

Road signs

The Highway Code has illustrations of all the traffic signs. Signs which give orders are mostly circular; warning signs are mostly triangular; direction signs are mostly rectangular; and information signs are all rectangular.

Sign spotting Make a note of how many different traffic signs you can see on a journey.

Sign census Make a list of all traffic signs, and find out how many of each you see on a particular journey.

Sign Snap Copy each traffic sign on to a piece of thin card about half the size of a playing card to make your own pack of traffic sign cards. You can then play this game, which can be played by any number of players.

How to play

1 Shuffle the cards.

2 Deal six cards to each player, and place any remaining face down, or in a box, as the central 'pool'.

3 Each player looks at all his cards.

4 Each time a player sees a sign beside the road which is the same as one in his hand, he says 'snap' and places that card at the bottom of the pool pile.

5 At any time a player can exchange *one* of his cards for *two* from the pool. The one he discards is placed at the bottom of the pool pile; the two he picks up are taken from the top of the pool pile.

6 The first player with no cards left is the winner.

ıns giving orders – mostly circular

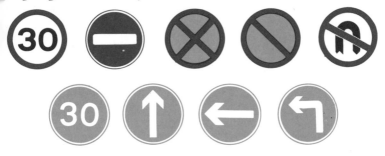

arning signs – mostly triangular

irection signs – mostly rectangular

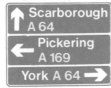

nformation signs – all rectangular

Vehicle index marks from October 1974 (see p.13)

AA	Bournemouth	CU	Newcastle	FO	Gloucester	JT	Bournemouth
AB	Worcester	CV	Truro	FP	Leicester	JU	Leicester
AC	Coventry	CW	Preston	FR	Preston	JV	Lincoln
AD	Gloucester	CX	Huddersfield	FS	Edinburgh	JW	Birmingham
AE	Bristol	CY	Swansea	FT	Newcastle	JX	Huddersfield
AF	Truro			FU	Lincoln	JY	Exeter
AG	Hull	DA	Birmingham	FV	Preston		
AH	Norwich	DB	Manchester	FW	Lincoln	KA-KD	Liverpool
AJ	Middlesbrough	DC	Middlesbrough	FX	Bournemouth	KE	Maidstone
AK	Sheffield	DD	Gloucester	FY	Liverpool	KF	Liverpool
AL	Nottingham	DE	Haverfordwest			KG	Cardiff
AM	Swindon	DF-DG	Gloucester	GA-GB	Glasgow	KH	Hull
AN	Reading	DH	Dudley	GC	London SW	KJ-KR	Maidstone
AO	Carlisle	DJ	Liverpool	GD-GE	Glasgow	KS	Edinburgh
AP	Brighton	DK	Manchester	GF	London SW	KT	Maidstone
AR	Chelmsford	DL	Portsmouth	GG	Glasgow	KU	Sheffield
AS	Inverness	DM	Chester	GH-GK	London SW	KV	Coventry
AT	Hull	DN	Leeds	GL	Truro	KW	Sheffield
AU	Nottingham	DO	Lincoln	GM	Reading	KX	Luton
AV	Peterborough	DP	Reading	GN-GP	London SW	KY	Sheffield
AW	Shrewsbury	DR	Exeter	GR	Newcastle		
AX	Cardiff	DS	Glasgow	GS	Luton	LA-LF	London NW
AY	Leicester	DT	Sheffield	GT	London SW	LG	Chester
		DU	Coventry	GU	London SE	LH	London NW
BA	Manchester	DV	Exeter	GV	Ipswich	LJ	Bournemouth
BB	Newcastle	DW	Cardiff	GW-GY	London SE	LK-LR	London NW
BC	Leicester	DX	Ipswich			LS	Edinburgh
BD	Northampton	DY	Brighton	HA	Dudley	LT-LU	London NW
BE	Lincoln			HB	Cardiff	LV	Liverpool
BF	Stoke-on-Trent	EA	Dudley	HC	Brighton	LW-LY	London NW
BG	Liverpool	EB	Peterborough	HD	Huddersfield		
BH	Luton	EC	Preston	HE	Sheffield	MA-MB	Chester
BJ	Ipswich	ED	Liverpool	HF	Liverpool	MC-MH	London NE
BK	Portsmouth	EE	Lincoln	HG	Preston	MJ	Luton
BL	Reading	EF	Middlesbrough	HH	Carlisle	MK-MM	London NE
BM	Luton	EG	Peterborough	HJ-HK	Chelmsford	MO	Reading
BN	Manchester	EH	Stoke-on-Trent	HL	Sheffield	MP	London NE
BO	Cardiff	EJ	Bangor	HM	London C	MR	Swindon
BP	Portsmouth	EK	Liverpool	HN	Middlesbrough	MS	Edinburgh
BR	Newcastle	EL	Bournemouth	HO	Bournemouth	MT-MU	London NE
BS	Inverness	EM	Liverpool	HP	Coventry	MV	London SE
BT	Leeds	EN	Manchester	HR	Swindon	MW	Swindon
BU	Manchester	EO	Preston	HS	Glasgow	MX-MY	London SE
BV	Preston	EP	Swansea	HT-HU	Bristol		
BW	Oxford	ER	Peterborough	HV	London C	NA-NF	Manchester
BX	Haverfordwest	ES	Dundee	HW	Bristol	NG	Norwich
BY	London NW	ET	Sheffield	HX	London C	NH	Northampton
		EU	Bristol	HY	Bristol	NJ	Brighton
CA	Chester	EV	Chelmsford			NK	Luton
CB	Manchester	EW	Peterborough	JA	Manchester	NL	Newcastle
CC	Bangor	EX	Norwich	JB	Reading	NM	Luton
CD	Brighton	EY	Bangor	JC	Bangor	NN	Nottingham
CE	Peterborough			JD	London C	NO	Chelmsford
CF	Reading	FA	Stoke-on-Trent	JE	Peterborough	NP	Worcester
CG	Bournemouth	FB	Bristol	JF	Leicester	NR	Leicester
CH	Nottingham	FC	Oxford	JG	Maidstone	NS	Glasgow
CJ	Gloucester	FD	Dudley	JH	Reading	NT	Shrewsbury
CK	Preston	FE	Lincoln	JJ	Maidstone	NU	Nottingham
CL	Norwich	FF	Bangor	JK	Brighton	NV	Northampton
CM	Liverpool	FG	Brighton	JL	Lincoln	NW	Leeds
CN	Newcastle	FH	Gloucester	JM	Reading	NX	Dudley
CO	Exeter	FJ	Exeter	JN	Chelmsford	NY	Cardiff
CP	Huddersfield	FK	Dudley	JO	Oxford		
CR	Portsmouth	FL	Peterborough	JP	Liverpool	OA-OC	Birmingham
CS	Glasgow	FM	Chester	JR	Newcastle	OD	Exeter
CT	Lincoln	FN	Maidstone	JS	Inverness	OE-ON	Birmingham